LINE BY LINE
SCOTLAND

NEIL GIBSON

AMBERLEY

First published 2021

Amberley Publishing
The Hill, Stroud
Gloucestershire, GL5 4EP

www.amberley-books.com

Copyright © Neil Gibson, 2021

The right of Neil Gibson to be identified as
the Author of this work has been asserted in
accordance with the Copyrights, Designs and
Patents Act 1988.

ISBN 978 1 3981 0464 8 (print)
ISBN 978 1 3981 0465 5 (ebook)

British Library Cataloguing in Publication Data.
A catalogue record for this book is available from
the British Library.

Typesetting by SJmagic DESIGN SERVICES, India.
Printed in Great Britain.

Contents

Introduction

Welcome to my collection of images showcasing my travels around the railways of
Scotland between 2000 to 2019. The book travels from the south along the coastal
section of the East Coast Main line and the rolling hills of the West Coast Main line,
through the central belt and up various routes to the rugged and majestic Highlands.
I have included as many of my favourite images as I could from numerous trips to
Scotland over the period. Scotland is always my number one destination to head for,
with time spent north of the border only limited by family activities, work holidays
and poor weather forecasts, but we all know how reliable they can be!

   I was born in Doncaster in the 1970s and grew up with an older brother, Geoff,
who had an interest in railways and worked at 'The Plant'. Early railway memories
centre around Doncaster and York, often including riding behind the mighty Deltics.
As I got older, we began to explore much of the UK by rail and my interest in
photography was born.

   Early cameras were handed down from my brother, along with the advice to always
use slide film. I can recall two different Minolta's before moving on to a Canon A1 and
then many Canon EOS3's (I still have three in a drawer) until moving on to digital full
time in 2010. I started my digital adventure with a Canon 400D, which was used in a
frame alongside the EOS 3 taking slides. Once the decision to go digital full time was

made, I upgraded to a Canon 5D Mk II and finally moved on to the Mk III, which I am still using today. The vast majority of my images are taken using a 50 mm standard lens but I also carry a 24–105 mm zoom along with 85 mm and 100 mm primes. The biggest change to my photography approach came in September 2014 when I began to experiment with using a pole and tablet connected via Wi-Fi to remotely operate the camera. I appreciate there are many different views on the use of poles and while I find it to be a pain to set up and operate on occasions, the many new vantage points that are opened up more than make up for the niggles.

My love affair with Scotland dates back to birth. My earliest family holiday memories are of trips to Perthshire, often staying near Pitlochry, and the holidays continued right through my childhood. Railway photography offers many opportunities to explore a large part of Scotland but I also head north on family holidays and weekends away with Sue, my wife, and Holly, our dog.

I regularly go through various websites to highlight potential opportunities to head off around the country, chasing rail tours and land cruises as well as keeping up to date with changes in workings and motive power. A photography trip will often start with phone calls between friends to see who is available, who can drive and what may be included in the itinerary. Planning and research can be extremely thorough, consulting previous images, OS maps and more recently utilising Google Earth and sun angle apps. Many trips start with a very early alarm call followed by a long drive as the sun begins to crest the horizon. For me nothing beats arriving at the chosen location in the highlands to find a clear, sunny day and breathing in the fresh, crisp air with its unmistakable aroma – magical!

In 2007 I created my website 'Travels with the Railway Obsessive' to share my results, the title being the perfect description for my interaction with the hobby of railway photography. I travel the length and breadth of the UK, often getting up at silly o'clock in search of the perfect image. When a planned trip leads to a great result there is no better feeling. I also enjoy the days out, visiting interesting and spectacular parts of the country, often in the company of good friends.

I always feel something is pulling me north to Scotland and the number of visits I make each year shows I give in regularly. With the railway scene constantly evolving there is always something new to go for and it's safe to say I will be back soon.

I would like to dedicate this book to my dear brother Geoff, who started me off on this crazy hobby, and to all the friends I've travelled with along the way.

Central Scotland

Immaculate in WCRC maroon livery, 31190 and 37261 pass Park Farm at Linlithgow on 1H95 13.40 Edinburgh–Spean Bridge 'Royal Scotsman', 14 May 2005.

DRS 66407 rounds the curve to Gleneagles on 4A66 08.40 Grangemout–Aberdeen intermodal, 12 February 2008.

EWS-liveried 67019 passes Blackford on 1Z67 06.30 York–Perth 'Northern Belle', 29 May 2009.

DRS 66416 nears Blackford on 4N47 13.10 Inverness–Grangemouth 'Tesco Express' on 17 October 2009.

An unidentified HST crosses the Forth bridge at North Queensferry on 1A87 17.10 Haymarket–Aberdeen, 14 July 2019.

Immaculately turned out in 'as delivered' blue/grey livery, 43006 passes Pettycur on 1Z43 09.46 Edinburgh–Inverness 'Let's Go Round Again' LNER HST finale charter, 18 December 2019.

East Coast Main Line

In faded Railfreight distribution livery 90027 heads up the branch from Drem Junction on the rear of 2Y12 11.34 Edinburgh–North Berwick, 2 May 2005.

Carrying revised Railfreight distribution livery, 90022 heads up the branch from Drem Junction on 2Y02 12:34 Edinburg–North Berwick, 2 May 2005.

GNER-liveried 91115 rounds the curve passing Houndwood on 1S09 09.00 LKX–Glasgow Central, 14 April 2006.

With a great cloudscape out over the North Sea, 91103 passes Marshall Meadows on 1D32 11.30 LKX–Edinburgh, 14 April 2006.

GNER-liveried 91130 runs along the famous cliffs section passing Lamberton on 1S17 13.00 LKX–Glasgow Central, 19 July 2006.

EWS-liveried 60051 runs through the flowering gorse passing Lamberton on 6E30 13.33 Dalzell–Lackenby empty steel, 14 April 2006.

With a threatening sky about to put a dampener on the day EWS-liveried 37410 passes Spital on 6B41 08.10 Powderhall–Oxwellmains 'binliner', 6 April 2007.

EWS-liveried 67007 arrives at Edinburgh Waverley on 1M16 20.38 Inverness–London Euston 'Caledonian Sleeper', 07 March 2009.

Cross Country-liveried 43321 passes East Linton on 1V47 10.05 Edinburgh–Penzance, 11 April 2009.

Malcolm Rail-liveried, DRS-operated 66412 passes Cockburnspath on the diverted 4S49 07.15 Daventry–Grangemouth intermodal, 11 April 2009.

National Express-liveried 43238 passes Houndwood on 1S19 14.00 LKX–Aberdeen, 11 April 2009.

DRS-liveried 37607 heads along the North Berwick branch past Fenton Barns on 1Q18 06.55 Millerhill–Heaton CS test train, 22 April 2009.

National Express-liveried 43305 runs through the gorse at Lamberton on 1S15 12.00 LKX–Inverness, 22 April 2009.

On hire to East Coast from Cross Country, 43303 passes Lamberton on 1E08 09.30 Edinburgh–LKX, 19 August 2010.

National Express-liveried but East Coast-branded 43309 passes Fairnieside on 1E10 07.52 Aberdeen–LKX, 19 August 2010.

DRS 66413 runs along the cliffs past Lamberton on the diverted 4M16 04.58 Grangemouth–Daventry intermodal, 30 April 2011.

Carrying a fresh coat of East Coast grey, 91103 passes Houndwood on 1S11 10.00 LKX–Edinburgh, 30 April 2011.

EWS-liveried 66164 rounds the bends at Houndwood on the diverted 4S43 06.10 Rugby–Mossend 'Tesco Express', 30 April 2011.

East Coast grey-liveried 43305 passes Horn Burn on 1S11 10.00 LKX–Aberdeen, 19 April 2014.

East Coast grey-liveried 91132 passes Horn Burn on 1S13 10.44 LKX–Edinburgh, 19 April 2014.

East Coast-branded 43320 runs along the North Sea past Burnmouth on 1E20 15.00 Edinburgh–Newark North Gate, 19 April 2014. The stock is carrying ex-MML livery but with East Coast branding.

East Coast grey-liveried 91132 passes Grantshouse loop on 1S18 13.00 LKX–Edinburgh, 21 May 2014.

In stunning winter sunshine and amazing light clarity East Coast grey 43314 runs along the cliffs past Lamberton on 1E13 07.55 Inverness–LKX, 5 December 2014.

Virgin Trains 91118 passes Houndwood on 1S15 11.30 LKX–Edinburgh, 17 August 2016.

Fresh off overhaul and repaint 43305 rounds the bends at Houndwood on 1S16 12.00 LKX–Inverness, 17 August 2016.

Flying Scotsman-liveried 91101 passes Houndwood on 1S18 13.00 LKX–Edinburgh, 17 August 2016.

Virgin Trains 43318 runs alongside the North Sea past Burnmouth on 1S22 15.00 LKX–Stirling, 17 August 2016.

GBRF 66740 runs along the cliffs past Burnmouth on 6E45 08.07 Fort William–North Blyth Alcan tanks, 17 August 2016.

With the remnants of the snow from the 'beast from the east' still visible Virgin Trains 43367 passes the start of Grantshouse loop on 1E15 09.52 Aberdeen–LKX, 9 March 2018.

A little later in the day and with the snow beginning to melt Cross Country-liveried 43384 passes Grantshouse on 1V64 13.07 FO Edinburgh–Plymouth, 9 March 2018.

Virgin Trains 43277 passes Grantshouse loop on 1S11 10.00 LKX–Aberdeen, 9 March 2018.

Virgin Trains 91132 passes Grantshouse loop on 1S13 11.00 LKX–Edinburgh, 9 March 2018.

Virgin Trains 'Spirit of Sunderland' 43274 runs through the delightful Scottish Borders past Horseley on 1S16 12.00 LKX–Inverness, 9 March 2018.

Virgin Trains 43314 passes Marshall Meadows on 1E05 07.30 Edinburgh–LKX, 19 April 2018.

Virgin Trains 43317 runs along the cliffs past Lamberton on 1E07 08.30 Edinburgh–LKX, 19 April 2018.

National Railway Museum-liveried 43238 passes Horn Burn on 1E13 07.55 Inverness–LKX, 19 April 2018.

With St Abbs head sticking out into the North Sea, 43312 passes Innerwick on 1S16 12.00 LKX–Inverness, 19 April 2018.

EWS-liveried but with DB branding 66002 stands in Grantshouse loop waiting time on the diverted 4M30 08.14 Grangemouth–Daventry intermodal, 5 May 2018.

National Railway Museum-liveried 43238 passes Grantshouse loop on 1E15 09.52 Aberdeen–LKX, 5 May 2018.

Virgin Trains 91105 runs through a sea of yellow gorse passing Lamberton on 1S15 11.30 LKX–Edinburgh, 5 May 2018.

Virgin Trains 91131 runs through a sea of gorse passing Houndwood on 1S09 09.00 LKX–Edinburgh, 16 May 2018.

Virgin Trains 43307 passes a carpet of yellow gorse at Houndwood on 1E15 09.52 Aberdeen–LKX, 16 May 2018.

Virgin Trains 43316 passes Houndwood on 1S11 10.00 LKX–Aberdeen, 16 May 2018.

Virgin Trains 91109 passes Penmanshiel on 1S18 13.00 LKX–Edinburgh, 16 May 2018.

With Ayton Castle on the skyline 91122 passes Cocklaw on 1S07 08.00 LKX–Edinburgh, 25 August 2018.

Celebrity 'Battle of Britain'-liveried 91110 passes Innerwick on 1S15 11.30 LKX–Edinburgh, 25 August 2018.

LNER red 91102 runs along the coast past Lamberton on 1S21 14.30 LKX–Edinburgh, 25 August 2018.

LNER red 43251 passes Prenderguest on 1E13 07.55 Inverness–LKX, 13 April 2019.

LNER red 91129 winds its way north past Cocklaw on 1S09 09.00 LKX–Edinburgh, 19 April 2019.

LNER red 43311 runs through Penmanshiel Wood on 1E17 09.40 SuO Inverness–LKX, 21 April 2019.

Network Rail yellow 43013 runs along the cliffs past Lamberton on 1Q23 10.38 Heaton–Edinburgh–Newcastle 'New Measurement Train', 29 April 2019.

When everything comes together – weather, loco and working. InterCity-liveried 91119 runs along the cliffs past Lamberton on 1S18 13.00 LKX–Edinburgh, 29 April 2019.

43272 passes Burnmouth on 1S22 15.00 LKX–Stirling, 6 May 2019.

After nailing this working at Sunderland Bridge near Durham earlier in the day we chose to chase up along the coast, and I'm very glad we made the decision. 56105 and 56096 thunder past the cliffs at Lamberton on 6Z31 Doncaster Up Decoy–Millerhill engineers, 28 June 2019.

LNER 43313 passes Reston in the Scottish borders on 1E13 07.55 Inverness-LKX, 07 September 2019.

Highland Main Line

National Express-liveried 43305 passes Balsporran Cottages, south of Dalwhinnie, on 1S15 12.00 LKX–Inverness, 29 May 2009.

DRS 66432 passes Crubenmore on 4H47 05.00 Grangemouth–Inverness 'Tesco Express', 30 May 2009.

DRS 37611 runs alongside the River Garry south of Dalnaspidal with failed 66432 DIT on 4N47 13.10 Inverness–Grangemouth 'Tesco Express', 30 May 2009.

DRS 66416 heads south from Pitlochry on 4N47 13.10 Inverness–Grangemouth 'Tesco Express', 17 October 2009.

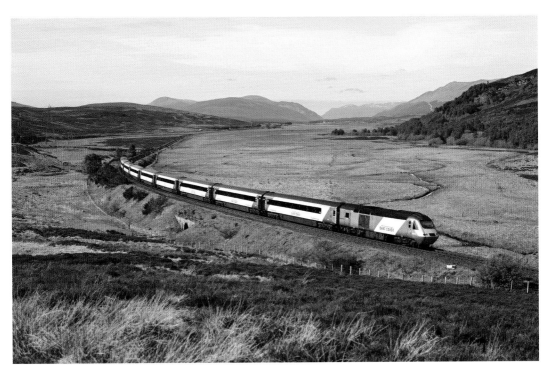

National Express-liveried but carrying East Coast branding 43308 passes Crubenmore on the rear of 1E12 07.55 Inverness–LKX, 3 June 2010

During the short period this train was operated by DB, 66099 passes Slochd at walking pace on its way to the summit pulling 4D47 13.23 Inverness–Mossend 'Tesco Express', 18 June 2010.

National Express-liveried but carrying East Coast branding 43251 departs Carrbridge on 1S15 12.00 LKX–Inverness, 19 June 2010.

In a very brief spell of morning sunshine National Express-liveried but carrying East Coast branding 43277 nears Balsporran Cottages, just south of Dalwhinnie, on 1E12 07.55 Inverness–LKX, 4 September 2010.

WCR-liveried 57001 begins its climb to the highlands, passing Dalmarnock on 1H89 13.41 Edinburgh–Dalwhinnie 'Royal Scotsman', 27 July 2011.

DRS 66421 runs alongside the A9 road passing Ballinluig on 4D47 13.14 Inverness–Mossend 'Tesco Express', 15 August 2011.

With the frost slowly clearing Freightliner 66601 passes Cuaich on 6H51 03.13 Oxwellmains–Inverness cement, 22 March 2012.

DRS 66304 crests Slochd Summit on 4H47 13.14 Inverness–Mossend 'Tesco Express', 25 May 2012.

DRS 66304 passes Dalnacardoch on 4H47 13.14 Inverness–Mossend 'Tesco Express', 25 May 2012.

DRS 66429 passes Coilintuie on 4H47 05.04 Mossend–Inverness 'Tesco Express', 17 April 2017.

Colas-liveried 37421 passes Crubenmore on 1Q79 14.55 Inverness–Mossend test train, 17 April 2017.

Virgin Trains-liveried and carrying 'Spirit of Sunderland' branding 43274 nears Dalwhinnie on 1S16 12.00 LKX–Inverness, 17 April 2017.

Looking smart in DB red livery, 67013 nears Wades Bridge, Dalwhinnie on 1S25 21.16 London Euston–Inverness 'Caledonian Sleeper', 4 May 2017.

Colas-liveried 60002 passes Cuaich on 6H51 02.43 Oxwellmains–Inverness cement, 4 May 2017.

68023 rounds the 's' bends towards Balsporran Cottages on 4H47 05.04 Mossend–Inverness 'Tesco Express', 4 May 2017.

Virgin Trains-liveried 43367 passes Crubenmore on 1E13 08.13 Inverness–LKX, 4 May 2017.

66743 passes along the River Garry at Dalnaspidal on 1H82 13.15 Kingussie–Dundee 'Royal Scotsman', 4 May 2017.

With a little afternoon cloud bubbling up and threatening the sun, 68023 crests Drumochter Summit on 4D47 13.05 Inverness–Mossend 'Tesco Express', 4 May 2017.

Looking smart in DB red livery, 67013 passes Cuaich on 1S25 21.16 London Euston–Inverness 'Caledonian Sleeper', 5 May 2017.

68023 heads south from Dalwhinnie on 4D47 13.05 Inverness–Mossend 'Tesco Express', 5 May 2017.

Saltire-liveried 170418 passes Dalnaspidal on 1H13 13.34 Edinburgh–Inverness, 5 May 2017.

DB red-liveried 67013 runs through the pass at Drumochter on 1S25 21.16 London Euston–Inverness 'Caledonian Sleeper', 6 May 2017.

68023 heads north from Drumochter on 4H47 05.04 Mossend–Inverness 'Tesco Express', 6 May 17.

68023 passes Crubenmore on 4H47 05.04 Mossend–Inverness 'Tesco Express', 6 May 2017.

Virgin Trains-liveried 43367 crests Drumochter Summit on 1E13 07.55 Inverness–LKX, 6 May 2017.

DRS 66422 sets off from its booked stop at Dalwhinnie on 4H47 05.04 Mossend–Inverness 'Tesco Express', 2 August 2017.

Colas-liveried 60076 crosses Slochd Viaduct on 6B31 11.05 Inverness–Oxwellmains empty cement, 2 August 2017.

In a remarkably lucky patch of sunlight Colas-liveried 37219 heads north through Glen Garry towards Dalnaspidal on 1Q77 13.00 Mossend–Inverness test train, 2 August 2017.

Colas-liveried 37421 passes Invereen on the rear of 1Q77 13.00 Mossend–Inverness test train, headed by 37219, 2 August 2017.

I love the highland air on a sunny morning. EWS-liveried 67007 pulls away from Dalwhinnie on 1S66 21.20 LKX–Inverness 'Caledonian Sleeper', 22 April 2019.

My take on an old classic shot made possible with the pole to get over the wires. DRS 66301 nears Wades Bridge as it approaches Dalwhinnie on 4H47 05.04 Mossend–Inverness 'Tesco Express', 22 April 2019.

DRS operated and carrying retro 'large logo' livery 37402 and 37409 make a splendid sight as they climb towards the summit at Drunochter on 1Z29 09.10 Aviemore–Eastleigh 'Easter Highlander' charter, 22 April 2019.

Kyle

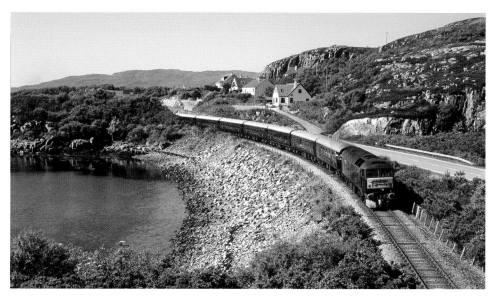

WCRC 47854 nears its destination, passing Badicaul on 1H80 08.00 Keith–Kyle of Lochalsh 'Royal Scotsman' 9 June 2006.

WCRC 47854 breaks the early morning quiet passing the delightful Badicaul on 1H81 08.45 Kyle of Lochalsh–Carrbridge 'Royal Scotsman', 9 June 2007.

WCRC 47854 passes Craigton on 1H81 08.45 Kyle of Lochalsh–Carrbridge 'Royal Scotsman', 9 June 2007.

WCRC 47854 near Luib on 1H81 08.45 Kyle of Lochalsh–Carrbridge 'Royal Scotsman', 9 June 2007.

WCRC 47854 runs alongside Loch a'Chuilinn on 1H81 08.45 Kyle of Lochalsh–Carrbridge 'Royal Scotsman' 9 June 2007.

After a lovely day spent in the west highlands the return chase began. EWS-liveried 37406 and 37410 pass Badicaul on 1Z30 18.15 Kyle of Lochalsh–Inverness charter, 9 June 2007.

37406 and 37410 are seen for a second time as they near Attadale on 1Z30 18.15 Kyle of Lochalsh–Inverness, 9 June 2007.

The third and final image on a wonderful evening, 37406 and 37410 near Achnasheen on 1Z30 18.15 Kyle of Lochalsh–Inverness, 9 June 2007.

DRS 37608 and 37610 run along the banks of Loch a-Chuilinn on 1Z37 11.30 Inverness–Kyle of Lochalsh charter, 19 June 2010.

Colas-liveried 37421 brings up the rear of 1Q78 13.12 Inverness–Kyle of Lochalsh test train crossing bridge at the east end of Loch Achanalt, 16 April 2017.

After a full dose of four seasons in one hour's weather, DRS 37259 and 37605 run alongside Loch Gowan on 1Z37 09.13 Inverness–Kyle of Lochalsh 'Easter Highlander', 1 April 2018.

DRS 37605 and 37259 catch a lucky patch of sun passing Badicaul on 1Z38 17.20 Kyle of Lochalsh–Inverness 'Easter Highlander', 1 April 2018.

DRS 37605 and 37259 glint in the evening sun passing Fodderty on 1Z38 17.20 Kyle of Lochalsh–Inverness 'Easter Highlander', 1 April 2018.

73969 and 73968 run along the edge of Loch a'Chuilinn on the rear of 1Z73 05.00 Paisley–Kyle of Lochalsh 'SRPS charter', 9 June 2018.

With the promise of a few breaks in the cloud I made the move towards the coast, resulting in this excellent image. 73967 and 73966 head away from Drumbuie on 1Z73 05.00 Paisley–Kyle of Lochalsh 'SRPS charter', 9 June 2018.

Attempt number three of this working and finally some sunshine. 37409 and 37419 pass Attadale on 1Z59 10.06 Aviemore–Kyle of Lochalsh 'Autumn Highlander', 28 September 2019.

Mallaig

One of my favourite images of all time. 50031 passes Kinloid on 5Z24 12.36 Mallaig–Arisaig–Mallaig stock shunt, 5 March 2005. I liked the nice touch on the large logo livery, the hood carrying the West Highland terrier logo.

In a torrential down pour and with a small rainbow just about visible 50031 crosses Loch Nan Umah Viaduct on 1Z24 14.40 Mallaig–Fort William, 5 March 2005. I'm amazed how well this turned out as the camera had to be kept out of the driving rain until the very last second.

DRS 37059 nears Glenfinnan station on 6K21 12.30 Fort William–Arisaig ballast drop, 22 March 2012.

DRS 37059 heads west from Glenfinnan on 6K21 12.30 Fort William–Arisaig ballast drop, 22 March 2012.

The second ballast drop for 37059 as it crawls past Polnish on 6K21 12.30 Fort William–Arisaig, 22 March 2012.

DRS 37059 pulls away from Polnish on 6K21 12.30 Fort William–Arisaig ballast drop, 22 March 2012.

The final pic of an incredible day, DRS 37059 crossing Loch Nan Umah Viaduct on 6K22 17.30 Arisaig–Fort William empty ballast, 22 March 2012.

37685 crosses Loch Nan Umah Viaduct on 1H86 08.23 Spean Bridge–Mallaig–Fort William 'Royal Scotsman', 26 May 2012.

37685 crosses the causeway at Loch Eilt on 1H86 08.23 Spean Bridge–Mallaig–Fort William 'Royal Scotsman', 26 May 2012.

DRS 37419 passes Loch Dubh on 6K60 10.40 Mallaig–Glenfinnan ballast drop, 26 February 2013.

DRS 37419 passes Drumsallie on 6K60 12.48 Glenfinnan–Fort William empty ballast, 26 February 2013.

WCRC-operated 37685 passes Kinloid on 1Q48 10.00 Fort William–Mossend via Mallaig, 26 March 2014. 37685 was hired after the failure of DRS 37259, which had a speedo fault.

DRS 37610 passes over the causeway at Loch Eilt on the rear of 1Q48 10.00 Fort William–Mossend via Mallaig, 26 March 2014. The train was headed by WCRC 37685.

With the snow-capped Ben Nevis range in the distance, DRS 37610 passes Drumsallie on the rear of 1Q48 10.00 Fort William–Mossend via Mallaig, 26 March 2014. The train was headed by WCRC 37685.

55003 (55022) passes the delightful scenery of Kinloid on 1H86 08.23 Spean Bridge–Fort William 'Royal Scotsman', 2 May 2015.

55003 (55022) powers away from Fort William on 1H86 08.23 Spean Bridge–Fort William 'Royal Scotsman', 9 May 2015.

55003 (55022) passes the delightful scenery of Kinloid at the rear of 1H86 08.23 Spean Bridge–Fort William 'Royal Scotsman', 9 May 2015.

55003 (55022) crosses the causeway at Loch Eilt on the rear of 1H86 08.23 Spean Bridge–Fort William 'Royal Scotsman', 9 May 2015

GBRF 66736 passes Loch Dubh on 1H86 08.23 Spean Bridge–Fort William 'Royal Scotsman', 23 April 2016.

This made the 3 a.m. alarm call worthwhile. 44871 crosses the magnificent Glenfinnan Viaduct on 2Y61 10.15 Fort William–Mallaig 'Jacobite', 1 October 2016.

With the train booked to stand in the station for thirty-five minutes we easily managed a second image. 44871 heads west from Glenfinnan on 2Y61 10.15 Fort William–Mallaig 'Jacobite', 1 October 2016.

DRS 37612 climbs away from Morar on 1Z53 13.25 Fort William–Mallaig 'Autumn Highlander', 1 October 2016. This was our second attempt at this train after being cruelly blocked by cloud at Loch Dubh.

DRS 37601 heads away from Mallaig on 2Z54 15.27 Mallaig–Arisaig 'Autumn Highlander', 1 October 2016.

Showing off the beautiful west highlands in all their glory, 156447 crosses Loch Nan Uamh Viaduct on 1Y43 14.24 Crianlarich–Mallaig, 1 October 2016.

Oban

WCRC-liveried 37248 runs through Glen Lochy on 1Z55 06.51 Newcastle–Oban rail tour, 5 May 2008.

DRS 37409 and 37423 run through Glen Lochy on 1Z90 07.23 Edinburgh–Oban 'Northern Belle', 3 September 2010.

After a chase from Glen Lochy DRS 37409 and 37423 pass Connel Ferry on 5Z90 13.18 Taynuilt–Oban ECS, 3 September 2010. Due to late running the passengers were taken off at Taynuilt to ensure they made the ferry connection from Oban to Mull.

73967 crosses the eastern end of Loch Awe on 5Y11 10.30 Oban–Polmadie 'Caledonian Sleeper', 27 February 2016. The train was running back to the depot ECS for servicing after a planned diversion to Oban due to the closure of the West Highland line to Fort William.

With the train booked to stop at Dalmally for seventy-five minutes to wait for the unit to pass we had plenty of time to move location. 73967 passes Dalrigh on 5Y11 10.30 Oban–Polmadie CS ECS, 27 February 2016.

DRS 37409 leads the Pathfinder Tours 'Easter Highlander' through Glen Lochy on 1Z40 09.30 Fort William–Oban charter, 24 April 2016.

37601 passes Succoth Lodge near Dalmally on 1Z56 09.27 Fort William–Oban 'Autumn Highlander', 2 October 2016.

After a very pleasant afternoon we found ourselves at Loch Awe as no other shots were on so late in the year. Thankfully the sun stayed above the hill for around a minute longer than we needed. 37612 crosses Loch Awe Viaduct on 1Z57 16.48 Oban–Fort William Pathfinder Tours 'Autumn Highlander', 2 October 2016.

73968 passes Succoth Lodge on the rear of the diverted 1Y11 04.50 Edinburgh–Oban 'Caledonian Sleeper', 25 March 2017.

73968 stands at Oban after arrival on the rear of the diverted 1Y11 04.50 Edinburgh–Oban 'Caledonian Sleeper', 25 March 2017.

73968 crosses Loch Awe Viaduct on 5Y11 10.30 Oban–Polmadie 'Caledonian Sleeper', 25 March 2017. The train is running back to the depot ECS for servicing after a planned diversion to Oban due to the closure of West Highland line to Fort William.

With the train booked a sixty-five-minute stop at Dalmally to pass the unit we wandered back up the valley for a second shot. 73968 passes the gallery at Dalrigh on 5Y11 10.30 Oban–Polmadie 'Caledonian Sleeper', 25 March 2017. The train is running back to the depot ECS for servicing after a planned diversion to Oban due to the closure of West Highland line to Fort William.

West Coast Main Line

GBRF-operated 87022 passes Crawford on 1M44 15.47 Shieldmuir–PRDC 325 mail unit drag, 10 May 2006.

Stobart-liveried 66414 *James the Engine crosses* the River Clyde bridge at Crawford on 4S43 06.12 Daventry–Grangemouth 'Tesco Express', 1 October 2009.

National Express-liveried 43320 crosses the River Clyde at Crawford on the diverted 1S02 06.08 Doncaster–Edinburgh, 17 October 2009.

EWS-liveried 92001 passes Greskine on 6O15 16.57 Mossend–Eastleigh 'enterprise', 3 June 2010.

First-liveried 90024 stands at Glasgow Central's platform 10 prior to departure on 1M11 23.55 Glasgow Central–London Euston 'Caledonian Sleeper', 26 January 2011.

92019 passes Lamington on 6V15 17.30 Mossend–Didcot 'Enterprise', 3 June 2011.

Freightliner 86613 and 86612 pass Greskine on 4M74 14.01 Coatbridge–Crewe BH liner, 21 April 2015.

325002, 325009 and 325013 pass Beattock Summit on 1M44 16.18 Shieldmuir–Warrington RMT, 21 April 2015.

Catching the last of the evening sun, Freightliner 86614 and 86632 pass Wandel on 4M11 17.34 Coatbridge–Crewe BH liner, 21 April 2015.

DRS operated and carrying retro 'large logo' livery 37402 and 37409 round the 'S' bends at Enterkenfoot on 1Z29 09.10 Aviemore–Eastleigh Pathfinder Tours 'Easter Highlander' charter, 22 April 2019.

88006 is seen passing Elvanfoot on 4S44 12.16 Daventry–Mossend intermodal, 20 September 2019.

West Highland Line

Perfectly timed as this was the only time the sun lit the scene while we were there. 50049 rounds the Horseshoe Curve on 1Z24 10.24 Fort William–Dalmuir, 6 March 2005.

EWS 37406 passes Achallader on 1Y11 04.50 Edinburgh–Fort William 'Caledonian Sleeper', 10 May 2006.

A scabby EWS-liveried 37405 rounds the Horseshoe Curve on 1Y11 04.50 Edinburgh–Fort William 'Caledonia Sleeper', 9 June 2006. This was the final booked class hauled 1Y11. It's a shame the loco's external condition did not reflect the occasion.

WCRC 37248 and DRS 37688 pass through Glen Falloch on 1Z56 16.22 Oban–Newcastle charter, 5 May 2008.

WCRC-operated 47786 heads north from Rannoch on 1H85 13.32 Edinburgh–Spean Bridge 'Royal Scotsman', 18 June 2010.

An unidentified Class 156 unit crosses the northern Horseshoe Curve viaduct on 1Y44 10.10 Mallaig–Crianlarich, 28 April 2012.

Standing in for the failed 57001, WCRC 37685 pulls away from Bridge of Orchy on 1H85 13.33 Edinburgh–Spean Bridge 'Royal Scotsman', 25 May 2012.

In perfect early morning conditions EWS 67004 passes Achallader on 1Y11 04.50 Edinburgh–Fort William 'Caledonian Sleeper', 30 March 2013.

DRS-liveried 37409 and 37607 blast north past Achallader on 1Z32 06.20 Paisley–Fort William Pathfinder Tours 'Easter Highlander', 30 March 2013.

After an overnight drive the sight of 'MELD' in the early morning sunshine brought a huge smile to the assembled gallery. 55003 (55022) passes Achnabobane on the rear of 1H86 08.23 Spean Bridge–Fort William 'Royal Scotsman', 2 May 2015.

WCRC 37516 nears County March Summit on 5Z51 06.05 Carnforth–Fort William Yard ECS, 9 May 2015. This working was one of the first to be operated by West Coast Railways after its temporary ban, conveying coaches for the Jacobite operation.

After waiting in the station for the unit to pass WCRC 37516 is seen again shortly after departing Bridge of Orchy on 5Z51 06.05 Carnforth–Fort William Yard ECS, 9 May 2015.

DRS-liveried 37409 and 37610 pass Achallader on 1Z40 09.30 Fort William–Oban Pathfinder Tours 'Easter Highlander', 24 April 2016.

Having almost given up and headed home due to the total blanket of cloud, we were amazed to nail this classic location. DRS-liveried 37610 and 37409 roar up the climb from Crianlarich, past Inverhaggernie, on 1Z41 16.45 Oban–Fort William Pathfinder Tours 'Easter Highlander', 24 April 2016.

DRS-liveried 37601 and 37612 pass Achallader on 1Z56 09.27 Fort William–Oban Pathfinder Tours 'Autumn Highlander', 2 October 2016.

With the West Highland line shots captured, it was time for a late afternoon drive out to Rannoch station in delightful conditions. GBRF 66737 crosses Rannoch Moor on 6S45 06.25 North Blyth Alcan–Fort William, 4 May 2017. For me this is as good as the hobby can get.

With the 'Tesco Express' due up the Highland main line running late, I decided to head west for another sleeper shot. 73966 crosses Rannoch Viaduct on 1Y11 04.50 Edinburgh–Fort William 'Caledonian Sleeper', 5 May 2017.

GBRF 66737 heads south from Rannoch across Garbh Ghaoir Viaduct on 6E45 08.07 Fort William–North Blyth Alcan empties, 5 May 2017.

With the superb conditions a second visit of the day to Rannoch had to be made. 66746 crosses Garbh Ghaoir Viaduct on 1H85 13.45 Edinburgh–Spean Bridge 'Royal Scotsman', 5 May 2017.